C000311058

What If
We Stopped
Pretending?

ALSO BY JONATHAN FRANZEN

NOVELS

Purity

Freedom

The Corrections

Strong Motion

The Twenty-Seventh City

NONFICTION

The End of the End of the Earth

Farther Away

The Discomfort Zone

How to Be Alone

The Kraus Project

What If We Stopped Pretending?

Jonathan Franzen

4th ESTATE • London

4th Estate
An imprint of HarperCollins*Publishers*
1 London Bridge Street
London SE1 9GF

www.4thEstate.co.uk

HarperCollins*Publishers*
1st Floor, Watermarque Building, Ringsend Road
Dublin 4, Ireland

First published in Great Britain in 2021 by 4th Estate

The essay "What If We Stopped Pretending?" first appeared in
the *New Yorker*, 8 September 2019. The interview by
Wieland Freund, "The Game Is Over", was first published in
Die Literarische Welt, 26 July 2019.

1

A catalogue record for this book is
available from the British Library

ISBN 978-0-00-843404-5

Set in Adobe Garamond Pro
Printed and bound in Great Britain by
CPI Group (UK) Ltd, Croydon

MIX
Paper from
responsible sources

FSC™ C007454

Contents

Foreword   1

What If We Stopped Pretending?   17

The Game Is Over.
Petro-consumerism Won   43

Foreword

On the third of June 2019, five months after the end of the driest year on record in Berlin and five months before the United States commenced its withdrawal from the Paris climate accord, I went out from Berlin to the little town of Jüterbog with my friend Andreas Meissner, the director of the Brandenburg Wilderness Foundation. The weather was extremely hot, and we stopped in town for a late lunch before venturing into the core area of the foundation's reserve at Jüterbog—a splendid expanse of regenerating forest that is home to wolves and otters and a number of breeding birds, such as nightjar and hoopoe, that are rare in northern Germany. Our plan was to spend the late afternoon and evening birdwatching.

As we entered the reserve, on a sandy track, we saw an angry column of smoke rising from the conifers ahead of us. Andreas got on the phone and learned that two trucks from the local fire department were already on the scene. We speeded farther down the track and came to a wide strip of land that the reserve managers had cleared as a fire break. The air temperature was nearly forty degrees. A strong, dry wind from the south was propelling the fire directly toward the fire trucks, which had stopped on the northern side of the break. Joining the firefighters, Andreas and I watched the black smoke billow toward us. Trees farther back in the forest were exploding into flame, their green boughs becoming wholly orange in the blink of an eye. At the last moment before the fire reached the break, I saw a woodlark shoot out from the woods and veer into the clearing, very probably abandoning her nest. Although the smoke and the heat were intense, the scariest thing was how fast the fire was moving. While Andreas and the firefighters and I retreated to a safer vantage point, the flames leaped right over the break and into the pine woods to the north.

There is very little wild forest left in northern Germany. By the time the Jüterbog fire was contained and extinguished, six hot days later, nearly 750 hectares had burned. I'd come to Berlin to talk about climate change and conservation—to argue that we shouldn't be so preoccupied with climate that we neglect the equally acute global crisis in biodiversity—but I found that the inferno I'd witnessed had complicated my argument. Although the fire couldn't be definitively attributed to climate change, the severity of the drought in Germany in 2018 and the intensity of the summer heat in 2019 were clearly harbingers of future calamities. I'd understood that our future is dark, but not until I saw those trees bursting into flame, saw how powerless the firefighters and the reserve managers were to contain the forces of nature, did I emotionally grasp how *fast* the calamities are approaching. The image that stayed with me was the speed.

When I returned home to California, whose wildfire problem is far more grievous than Germany's, I found that I needed to try again to write about climate change. With the image of the fire's speed fresh in mind, I needed to come to terms with the possibility that climate apocalypse would occur in my own lifetime. I'd written and spoken about the subject repeatedly in recent years, without feeling that my message had been understood, and I wanted to produce a concise summary of that message, necessarily darkened by what I'd experienced in Jüterbog.

Climate change had been on my radar for three decades. In 1992, I attended a lecture by a pair of plant physiologists who were hoping to reengineer the chlorophyll molecule and genetically implant it in food crops, to increase the efficiency of photosynthesis and make the crops more tolerant of drought, and in the course of their lecture they laid out a long and compelling story of the Earth's atmospheric carbon. Some years later, I borrowed and retold their story in a novel, *The Corrections*, and I enjoyed alarming my friends in New York with dire talk of global warming, but it wasn't until I fell in love with birds that I gave more sustained thought to it. The problem, for me, was partly that wild bird populations were likely to suffer as the planet warmed. But as I began to involve myself directly in bird conservation, I became aware of a different kind of problem: the environmental movement, which had formerly championed wild animals and plants, and had fought to preserve their habitat, had now been almost wholly captured by the issue of climate change. The major environmental groups were devoting most of their energy and resources to a single issue, on the theory that "if we don't stop climate change, nothing else will matter."

This emphasis had made sense in the 1990s, when there seemed to be a good chance that the world would take collective action to curtail carbon emissions. By 2015, however, it was clear to me that collective action had failed and would continue to fail. Meanwhile, what remained of the natural world was in worse trouble than ever, as every nation pursued economic growth at nature's expense, and I felt frustrated, as a bird lover, that the public environmental conversation continued to be so dominated by climate. Since this discourse seemed increasingly futile, I thought we should pay more attention to the natural world, where there were still meaningful and effective actions to be taken on its behalf.

The essay I published on the subject, in the *New Yorker*, was greeted by a flood of public hostility from the climate establishment and a trickle of gratitude from conservationists. I was heartened by the gratitude, but I came to feel that I'd invited the hostility by writing in a somewhat polemical tone. And so, in 2017, I wrote a second essay, adopting a more gentle and ironic approach, and published it in the *Guardian*. The response to the second essay seemed less heated, perhaps because not as many people read it, but it did eventually earn me a severe public scolding from the American climate activist Bill McKibben.

This might have been a good time for a novelist to retire from writing climate essays that upset people, but my experience of the Jüterbog fire coincided with the beginning of the presidential campaign season in America (a season that lasts nearly two years) and with an upsurge of climate activism in Europe. My old frustration—that people *still* weren't talking about the biodiversity crisis—was compounded by the new frustration of hearing American politicians and European activists repeat, at this very late date, when the apocalyptic fires had already begun, the same old platitudes. *We still have ten years. Let's get to work on saving the planet.*

The short essay I wrote wasn't intended as a polemic. I wanted to speak from the heart and try to answer, calmly, some of the questions I'd been asked about the earlier essays: *Are you saying we should simply give up on fighting climate change? Isn't a modest mitigation better than no mitigation at all? Isn't it politically counterproductive to deprive people of hope?* It seemed to me that, given the bleakness of our predicament, the problem of hope was crucial—a world-sized version of the problem of maintaining hope in the face of individual mortality—and that genuine hope insists on honesty and love. On honesty because hope is an investment like any other, best made with a clear eye. And on love because, without it, there's really nothing worth hoping for.

When the essay came out, again in the *New Yorker*, I realized that I might as well have written a polemic. The response of the climate establishment, mostly on social media, was ferociously negative. In a sense, I'd asked for it, by implying that the establishment is committed, in its own way, to denial of climate reality. Certainly I couldn't have asked for better evidence of the psychological force of that denial. Enraged climate journalists represented the essay to have said things it manifestly hadn't said, or to have omitted statements it had manifestly included. But, social media being what it is, much of the criticism was even more primitive. It didn't even matter what I'd said. To dismiss the essay, all you needed to know was that a privileged white man had written it. Or, if you were a climate scientist, that a non-scientist had written it.

The social-media response might have depressed me even more than our destruction of the planet—my own hopes lie not in averting climate catastrophe but in our capacity to deal with it reasonably and humanely—if I hadn't received, through other channels, an extraordinary volume of thanks and affirmation. It turns out that a lot of people, if they have no professional or political stake in activism, are thinking about climate as I do. A lot of people are dismayed by the erosion of civil discourse, are impatient with the obsolete promises of politicians and activists, are eager to make sense of our desperate situation, and are looking for ways to sustain some kind of hope.

These people give *me* hope, and it's to them that I dedicate this small book. To make it a little less laughably small, I'm including an interview I gave to Wieland Freund, for *Die Literarische Welt*. The interview with Wieland confirmed me in my resolve to write one last climate essay, and he has my gratitude for that.

Santa Cruz, 6 November 2019

What If
We Stopped
Pretending?

"There is infinite hope," Kafka tells us, "only not for us." This is a fittingly mystical epigram from a writer whose characters strive for ostensibly reachable goals and, tragically or amusingly, never manage to get any closer to them. But it seems to me, in our rapidly darkening world, that the converse of Kafka's quip is equally true: *There is no hope, except for us.*

I'm talking, of course, about climate change. The struggle to rein in global carbon emissions and keep the planet from melting down has the feel of Kafka's fiction. The goal has been clear for thirty years, and despite earnest efforts we've made essentially no progress toward reaching it. Today, the scientific evidence verges on irrefutable. If you're younger than sixty, you have a good chance of witnessing the radical destabilization of life on earth—massive crop failures, apocalyptic fires, imploding economies, epic flooding, hundreds of millions of refugees fleeing regions made uninhabitable by extreme heat or permanent drought. If you're under thirty, you're all but guaranteed to witness it.

If you care about the planet, and about the people and animals who live on it, there are two ways to think about this. You can keep on hoping that catastrophe is preventable, and feel ever more frustrated or enraged by the world's inaction. Or you can accept that disaster is coming, and begin to rethink what it means to have hope.

Even at this late date, expressions of unrealistic hope continue to abound. Hardly a day seems to pass without my reading that it's time to "roll up our sleeves" and "save the planet"; that the problem of climate change can be "solved" if we summon the collective will. Although this message was probably still true in 1988, when the science became fully clear, we've emitted as much atmospheric carbon in the past thirty years as we did in the previous two centuries of industrialization. The facts have changed, but somehow the message stays the same.

Psychologically, this denial makes sense. Despite the outrageous fact that I'll soon be dead forever, I live in the present, not the future. Given a choice between an alarming abstraction (death) and the reassuring evidence of my senses (breakfast!), my mind prefers to focus on the latter. The planet, too, is still marvelously intact, still basically normal—seasons changing, another election year coming, new comedies on Netflix—and its impending collapse is even harder to wrap my mind around than death. Other kinds of apocalypse, whether religious or thermo-nuclear or asteroidal, at least have the binary neatness of dying: one moment the world is there, the next moment it's gone forever. Climate apocalypse, by contrast, is messy. It will take the form of increasingly severe crises compounding chaotically until civilization begins to fray. Things will get very bad, but maybe not too soon, and maybe not for everyone. Maybe not for me.

Some of the denial, however, is more willful. The evil of the Republican Party's position on climate science is well known, but denial is entrenched in progressive politics, too, or at least in its rhetoric. The Green New Deal, the blueprint for some of the most substantial proposals put forth on the issue, is still framed as our last chance to avert catastrophe and save the planet, by way of gargantuan renewable-energy projects. Many of the groups that support those proposals deploy the language of "stopping" climate change, or imply that there's still time to prevent it. Unlike the political right, the left prides itself on listening to climate scientists, who do indeed allow that catastrophe is theoretically avertable. But not everyone seems to be listening carefully. The stress falls on the word *theoretically*.

Our atmosphere and oceans can absorb only so much heat before climate change, intensified by various feedback loops, spins completely out of control. Many scientists and policy-makers fear that we're in danger of passing this point of no return if the global mean temperature rises by more than two degrees Celsius (maybe more, but also maybe less). The I.P.C.C.—the Intergovernmental Panel on Climate Change—tells us that, to limit the rise to less than two degrees, we not only need to reverse the trend of the past three decades. We need to approach zero net emissions, globally, in the *next* three decades.

This is, to say the least, a tall order. It also assumes that you trust the I.P.C.C.'s calculations. New research, recently described in *Scientific American*, demonstrates that climate scientists, far from exaggerating the threat of climate change, have underestimated its pace and severity. To project the rise in the global mean temperature, scientists rely on complicated atmospheric modelling. They take a host of variables and run them through supercomputers to generate, say, ten thousand different simulations for the coming century, in order to make a "best" prediction of the rise in temperature. When a scientist predicts a rise of two degrees Celsius, she's merely naming a number about which she's very confident: the rise will be *at least* two degrees. The rise might, in fact, be far higher.

As a non-scientist, I do my own kind of modelling. I run various future scenarios through my brain, apply the constraints of human psychology and political reality, take note of the relentless rise in global energy consumption (thus far, the carbon savings provided by renewable energy have been more than offset by consumer demand), and count the scenarios in which collective action averts catastrophe. The scenarios, which I draw from the prescriptions of policy-makers and activists, share certain necessary conditions.

The first condition is that every one of the world's major polluting countries institute draconian conservation measures, shut down much of its energy and transportation infrastructure, and completely retool its economy. According to a recent paper in *Nature*, the carbon emissions from existing global infrastructure, if operated through its normal lifetime, will exceed our entire emissions "allowance"—the further gigatons of carbon that can be produced without crossing the threshold of catastrophe. (This estimate does not include the thousands of new energy and transportation projects already planned or under construction.) To stay within that allowance, a top-down intervention needs to happen not only *in* every country but *throughout* every country. Making New York City a green utopia will not avail if Texans keep pumping oil and driving pickup trucks.

The actions taken by these countries must also be the right ones. Vast sums of government money must be spent without wasting it and without lining the wrong pockets. Here it's useful to recall the Kafkaesque joke of the European Union's biofuel mandate, which served to accelerate the deforestation of Indonesia for palm-oil plantations, and the American subsidy of ethanol fuel, which turned out to benefit no one but corn farmers.

Finally, overwhelming numbers of human beings, including millions of government-hating Americans, need to accept high taxes and severe curtailment of their familiar life-styles without revolting. They must accept the reality of climate change and have faith in the extreme measures taken to combat it. They can't dismiss news they dislike as fake. They have to set aside nationalism and class and racial resentments. They have to make sacrifices for distant threatened nations and distant future generations. They have to be permanently terrified by hotter summers and more frequent natural disasters, rather than just getting used to them. Every day, instead of thinking about breakfast, they have to think about death.

* * *

Call me a pessimist or call me a humanist, but I don't see human nature fundamentally changing anytime soon. I can run ten thousand scenarios through my model, and in not one of them do I see the two-degree target being met.

To judge from recent opinion polls, which show that a majority of Americans (many of them Republican) are pessimistic about the planet's future, and from the success of a book like David Wallace-Wells's *The Uninhabitable Earth*, which was released in 2019, I'm not alone in having reached this conclusion. But there continues to be a reluctance to broadcast it. Some climate activists argue that if we publicly admit that the problem can't be solved, it will discourage people from taking any ameliorative action at all. This seems to me not only a patronizing calculation but an ineffectual one, given how little progress we have to show for it to date. The activists who make it remind me of the religious leaders who fear that, without the promise of eternal salvation, people won't bother to behave well. In my experience, nonbelievers are no less loving of their neighbors than believers. And so I wonder what might happen if, instead of denying reality, we told ourselves the truth.

First of all, even if we can no longer hope to be saved from two degrees of warming, there's still a strong practical and ethical case for reducing carbon emissions. In the long run, it probably makes no difference how badly we overshoot two degrees; once the point of no return is passed, the world will become self-transforming. In the shorter term, however, half measures are better than no measures. Halfway cutting our emissions would make the immediate effects of warming somewhat less severe, and it would somewhat postpone the point of no return. The most terrifying thing about climate change is the speed at which it's advancing, the almost monthly shattering of temperature records. If collective action resulted in just one fewer devastating hurricane, just a few extra years of relative stability, it would be a goal worth pursuing.

In fact, it would be worth pursuing even if it had no effect at all. To fail to conserve a finite resource when conservation measures are available, to needlessly add carbon to the atmosphere when we know very well what carbon is doing to it, is simply wrong. Although the actions of one individual have zero effect on the climate, this doesn't mean that they're meaningless. Each of us has an ethical choice to make. During the Protestant Reformation, when "end times" was merely an idea, not the horribly concrete thing it is today, a key doctrinal question was whether you should perform good works because it will get you into Heaven, or whether you should perform them simply because they're good—because, while Heaven is a question mark, you know that *this* world would be better if everyone performed them. I can respect the planet, and care about the people with whom I share it, without believing that it will save me.

More than that, a false hope of salvation can be actively harmful. If you persist in believing that catastrophe can be averted, you commit yourself to tackling a problem so immense that it needs to be everyone's overriding priority forever. One result, weirdly, is a kind of complacency: by voting for green candidates, riding a bicycle to work, avoiding air travel, you might feel that you've done everything you can for the only thing worth doing. Whereas, if you accept the reality that the planet will soon overheat to the point of threatening civilization, there's a whole lot more you should be doing.

Our resources aren't infinite. Even if we invest much of them in a longest-shot gamble, reducing carbon emissions in the hope that it will save us, it's unwise to invest all of them. Every billion dollars spent on high-speed trains, which may or may not be suitable for North America, is a billion not banked for disaster preparedness, reparations to inundated countries, or future humanitarian relief. Every renewable-energy mega-project that destroys a living ecosystem—the "green" energy development now occurring in Kenya's national parks, the giant hydroelectric projects in Brazil, the construction of solar farms in open spaces, rather than in settled areas— erodes the resilience of a natural world already fighting for its life. Soil and water depletion, overuse of pesticides, the devastation of world fisheries—collective will is needed for these problems, too, and, unlike the problem of carbon, they're within our power to solve. As a bonus, many low-tech conservation actions (restoring forests, preserving grasslands, eating less meat) can reduce our carbon footprint as effectively as massive industrial changes.

All-out war on climate change made sense only as long as it was winnable. Once you accept that we've lost it, other kinds of action take on greater meaning. Preparing for fires and floods and refugees is a directly pertinent example. But the impending catastrophe heightens the urgency of almost any world-improving action. In times of increasing chaos, people seek protection in tribalism and armed force, rather than in the rule of law, and our best defense against this kind of dystopia is to maintain functioning democracies, functioning legal systems, functioning communities. In this respect, any movement toward a more just and civil society can now be considered a meaningful climate action. Securing fair elections is a climate action. Combatting extreme wealth inequality is a climate action. Shutting down the hate machines on social media is a climate action. Instituting humane immigration policy, advocating for racial and gender equality, promoting respect for laws and their enforcement, supporting a free and independent press, reducing the number of assault weapons in circulation—these are all meaningful climate actions. To survive rising temperatures, every system, whether of the natural world or of the human world, will need to be as strong and healthy as we can make it.

And then there's the matter of hope. If your hope for the future depends on a wildly optimistic scenario, what will you do ten years from now, when the scenario becomes unworkable even in theory? Give up on the planet entirely? To borrow from the advice of financial planners, I might suggest a more balanced portfolio of hopes, some of them longer-term, most of them shorter. It's fine to struggle against the constraints of human nature, hoping to mitigate the worst of what's to come, but it's just as important to fight smaller, more local battles that you have some realistic hope of winning. Keep doing the right thing for the planet, yes, but also keep trying to save what you love *specifically*—a community, an institution, a wild place, a species that's in trouble—and take heart in your small successes. Any good thing you do now is arguably a hedge against the hotter future, but the really meaningful thing is that it's good today. As long as you have something to love, you have something to hope for.

In Santa Cruz, where I live, there's an organization called the Homeless Garden Project. On a small working farm at the west end of town, it offers employment, training, support, and a sense of community to members of the city's homeless population. It can't "solve" the problem of homelessness, but it's been changing lives, one at a time, for nearly thirty years. Supporting itself in part by selling organic produce, it contributes more broadly to a revolution in how we think about people in need, the land we depend on, and the natural world around us. In the summer, as a member of its community-supported agriculture program, I enjoy its kale and strawberries, and in the fall, because the soil is alive and uncontaminated, small migratory birds find sustenance in its furrows.

There may come a time, sooner than any of us likes to think, when the systems of industrial agriculture and global trade break down and homeless people outnumber people with homes. At that point, traditional local farming and strong communities will no longer just be liberal buzzwords. Kindness to neighbors and respect for the land—nurturing healthy soil, wisely managing water, caring for pollinators—will be essential in a crisis and in whatever society survives it. A project like the Homeless Garden offers me the hope that the future, while undoubtedly worse than the present, might also, in some ways, be better. Most of all, though, it gives me hope for today.

The Game Is Over. Petro-consumerism Won

The hockey stick graph depicting global mean temperature rise is 20 years old; "The Limits to Growth", the famous report by the Club of Rome, 47 years old; Rachel Carson's book *Silent Spring* is 57 years old. The ecological crisis could have been a dominant theme for decades, but—at least in Europe—it's becoming one only now. Why? *asks Wieland Freund.*

A point that I'm at pains to make is that "environmentalism" entails more than one thing —that there are many different ways of being green. Fighting climate change is certainly one of those ways. But the fact that climate is now a dominant theme in Europe doesn't mean that Europe has suddenly become environmentally conscious. European countries continue to wreak havoc on the natural world—through a sterilizing agricultural policy, through the destruction of fisheries, through forestry mismanagement, through wildly unsustainable levels of legal and illegal hunting, and, yes, through wind farms and biodiesel mandates and other "virtuous" energy programs—and very few people seem to be talking about any of that. To me, the sudden new preoccupation with climate suggests that most Europeans only care about the planet if they personally are threatened. And, of course, it's not just Europeans. Most Americans are the same way.

You write: "We're told that, as a species, human beings are hardwired to take the short view." Is *Homo sapiens* too stupid to tackle climate change?

Well, I was making fun of the word "hard-wired," a concept that originated in sociobiology and is flourishing in a time when computers are the preferred metaphor for describing the human brain. But your question puts me in mind of the great Karl Kraus line, "We were smart enough to build the machines and too stupid to make them serve us." The climate crisis isn't a matter of intelligence—an average eighth-grader can understand what our carbon emissions are doing to the atmosphere. What makes the crisis so daunting is that it can be understood in a variety of ways: as a failure of global governance, a failure to properly price carbon emissions, a contest between rich nations and poor nations, a gigantic collective-action dilemma, an ethics puzzle (how to accurately value harm to future generations), and so on. The climate crisis would have been difficult to overcome if it had consisted of even just one of those problems. When you multiply five different difficult problems together, as climate change does, you get a problem that no amount of intelligence can solve. Karl Kraus wasn't dissing the human brain. He was pointing to the ever-growing gap between technological progress and moral progress. As literature is in the business of reminding us, human nature progresses very slowly, if at all.

Your collection *The End of the End of the Earth* includes the essay "Save What You Love," which was hotly debated. You were called a climate denier and, among other insults, a "bird brain." What was your crime?

I just committed the crime again in my preceding answer, by using the past conditional tense: climate change *would have been* a difficult problem to solve. In other words, we failed to solve it, end of story. This opinion wasn't taken kindly by the many constituencies that have an interest in pretending that catastrophe can still be averted. Among those constituencies are the Democratic Party and the mainstream climate establishment in the United States. Almost every day, in the *New*

York Times, the voice of liberal America, some progressive politician or activist will issue another call to "get serious" about climate change and "save the planet." In truth, the time for getting serious was thirty years ago. The horse has left the barn! To publicly admit this, however, would be politically disastrous. Because the Republican Party pretends that there is no climate problem, the Democrats have to keep pretending that we can solve it—otherwise the dispute is purely academic. My crime against liberal orthodoxy was to not go along with that pretense.

If I'm not mistaken, you were mainly pointing out that, even without climate change,
unfortunately, human beings are causing a
massive extinction event. Certainly by the
time the United Nations report on mass
extinction was published, it should have been
clear that you were right. Where is the problem? Isn't it obvious that the acute ecological
crisis we're facing has more than one
dimension?

It should be obvious. But I invite you, if you
have time on your hands, to read the statements of the 2020 Democratic candidates for
U.S. president and see how many references
to extinctions you can find. Also notice, in
any press coverage of the extinction crisis, how

immediately the words "climate change" appear. The political voltage surrounding climate is so high that any other discussion of the natural world is instantly short-circuited. What infuriates me is that, unlike climate change, many of the threats to global biodiversity can be meaningfully reduced. Public discourse is dominated by a single problem, climate, which has no solution (at best, it can be somewhat mitigated), while there are equally pressing environmental problems that could actually be solved.

On the subject of climate change, there are indeed some hard, disillusioned sentences to be found in your work. Here's an example: "Our world is poised to change vastly, unpredictably, and mostly for the worse. I don't have any hope that we can stop the change from coming." The Paris treaty, the two-degree goal, Fridays for Future, and the pricing of CO_2: all too late?

Yes, too late. The I.P.C.C.—which has in any case been guilty, in the past, of massaging scientific data to produce more politically palatable predictions—suggests that it's still possible to keep global mean temperatures from rising more than 1.5 degrees. But to even have a chance of hitting that figure, every country in the world would have to entirely remake its infrastructure and economy in the next ten years. Maybe Sweden can become a net carbon non-emitter by 2030. But people in France are rioting over a minor gasoline tax, people in Trump America are in love with their pickup trucks, and let's not even talk about China and India and Africa, where yet another huge new coal-fired power plant comes on line every day. To me, it's an instance of the dark comedy of climate change that anyone can seriously imagine that the world will happily renounce the lifestyle benefits of economic growth. The game is over. Petro-consumerism won.

You're not worried that your argument plays into the hands of climate skeptics who want to leave everything as it is?

People who don't listen to climate science are the lowest of the low. I don't think they need my help to be vicious and ugly. I'm more interested in the "virtuous" side of the debate —the Green New Dealers, the Fridays for Future people. I hold them to a higher standard of honesty, and I want them to expand their definition of being green to include what we're doing to the other species on the planet; to talk a little less about climate and a little more about solvable problems. So far, only Extinction Rebellion has been willing to do this.

To be completely clear: you think it's absolutely necessary that we reduce CO_2. Regarding the fight against global warming, you write that "every half-degree counts." At the same time, you feel lied to and betrayed. Why?

Imagine that a friend of mine is smoking two packs of cigarettes a day. I might say to him, "Man, you've got to quit cigarettes, you're going to get cancer or emphysema. If you keep smoking, it's going to take years off your life." I love my friend, and I want him to live as long as possible. But then imagine the person who says to him, "If you quit cigarettes, you never have to die at all!" It is now all but certain that future climate change will be catastrophic. It's not quite as certain as the fact that we're all going to die, but it's getting there fast. (Interesting weather you've been having in Europe.) Naturally, we want to delay and mitigate the catastrophe as much as possible. The ethical exercise of reducing our carbon footprint is important; it's something to feel good about doing. But it's not the *only* thing worth doing, because it will no more avert the catastrophe than we can avert our own death. A better balanced life would consist of some large hopeless battles and some smaller battles that can be satisfyingly won.

But isn't it the case that many scientists assure us the climate crisis can still be averted? Why don't you believe them?

Read the fine print: if the climate scientist isn't also a lobbyist or an activist—in other words, if she's honest—she will specify that it's *theoretically* possible to avert the worst scenarios. And then go look at the list of countries that have resolved to leave their carbon in the ground. There are no countries on that list.

A politics of climate that's worthy of the name has basically not even started on a global scale. Where will the pressure come from? From the streets? From the top?

In the fantasy world of green-leftist politics—a binary world consisting of the wonderful, altruistic mass of humanity and the evil carbon-extraction industry that has it in its iron grip—the pressure will come from the street: kind-hearted people will naturally rise up and seize power, for the good of their grandchildren. In a less fantastical world, where people aren't quite so naturally far-sighted and selfless, the only hope of hitting the I.P.C.C.'s emissions numbers is the radical transformation of almost every aspect of daily life. Which would be, to put it mildly, socially disruptive. In America, the result might literally be a civil war.

Right now, it's young people who are protesting for a more aggressive climate policy. Is there a violent generational conflict in our future?

Oh, there's no question. I think we're beginning to see, within Western democracies, a replication of the conflict between wealthy carbon-emitting nations and the smaller, poorer nations that are going to be submerged by rising sea levels. An affluent seventy-year-old American has already done his damage to the atmosphere, and he doesn't have to experience the results of it. The people who will experience them are younger or far away, and they have every right to be angry about that. But—and here again, the literary point of view—this doesn't mean that they wouldn't have behaved exactly as the seventy-year-old American did, had their positions been reversed. Their complaint is legitimate, but it doesn't reflect an innate moral superiority.

Is humanity even capable of restraint?

People are more likely to exercise restraint if they see everyone else doing it. But it's so tempting for people to cheat.

If global warming in excess of two degrees is already a foregone conclusion, what should we do about its victims? Is it time to be talking about reparations?

I'm strongly in favor of reparations, but I can afford to be. Reparations are a tougher sell politically with the middle class and the working class in Western countries. I do think that when Bangladesh or the Seychelles is inundated there will be a global outpouring of compassion and support; the world will respond to images of distant suffering. The much, much more daunting problem is the billions of people now subsisting in regions susceptible to permanent drought and extreme high temperatures. The immigration pressure in the future will make the recent refugee crisis in Europe look like a Sunday picnic. I fear the outcome will be very ugly.

In the essay that opens *The End of the End of the Earth*, you offer a kind of coda to the controversial essay "Save What You Love." In the new essay, you seem to have regrets, not for what you said but for the tone in which you said it. You suggest that you should have considered the feelings of people who need more hope in their lives than you do. How do you give them courage after promising them a hot, calamitous future?

You might as well ask me how I get up in the morning, knowing I'll be dead soon. But that's an imperfect parallel, because the prospect of a hot, anarchic, extinction-filled future isn't quite as terrible to me as the prospect of being dead. Chaotic weather and rising sea levels are probably not an existential threat to the human species. The really serious threats arise from more deliberate applications of technology—nuclear weapons, recombinant DNA, and (if you believe in it) the Singularity. I'm sad about the planet, but I still get up in the morning and try to live well. I go to work, I appreciate life, and I do as much as I can for the people and the places and the animals I care about. Knowing that nothing lasts forever makes this more important, not less.

Can it be that struggling with insoluble problems is more difficult for us than for our ancestors? And, if so, why is that? And what can we learn from it?

Your question puts me in mind of the writers Steven Pinker and Guido Mingels, whose recent books make the case that the human condition has greatly improved in the past fifty years—globally, we're safer, healthier, less hungry, more prosperous, less violent, than ever before. I think Pinker and Mingels err in not considering the catastrophic cost of our success to other species, and their optimism about the future is grating to anyone who reads tragic literature. (As the financial prospectus says: "Past performance does not guarantee future results.") But their work is a useful reminder that, for most of the history of our species, *lots* of problems were insoluble—disease, crop failure, war, etc.—and that it's only in recent times that some of those problems have receded (for the moment). In other words, our current historical moment is a wild aberration. Insoluble problems are the fundamental human condition. Which is why I'm predicting a coming boom in literature.